Contents

Zoroku's adoptive father, Rokuichi, made this portrait of him.

Chapter 1
Samurai Sketching

Do you see pictures when you look at the world around you? Have you ever imagined that your eyes were paintbrushes and your mind was paper? Do you sometimes consider turning the sounds, sights, and scents you encounter in wild places into art? Creating art can open windows to nature's mysteries. It can unlock treasure chests full of questions and secret passages to discovery. Imagine spending your whole life tracking nature as a curious artist.

Over a century ago, a young Japanese boy began to draw the natural world around him. Though he was only five years old, Zoroku Sato was learning skills he would use for the rest of his life to picture the beauty, peace, and wildness he discovered outdoors. He was on his way to becoming a **naturalist,** a person who studies nature. Although many naturalists are scientists, Zoroku learned to explore nature through art.

Zoroku was born on November 18, 1885, on the Japanese island of Honshu. When he was five years old, he was adopted by his older brother, an artist named Rokuichi, and his wife, Kichiko. Rokuichi and Kichiko were unable to have children of their own, and at that time in Japan, it was fairly common for an older brother to adopt a younger one.

Kichiko's family, the Obatas, had been **samurai** for generations. Samurai were warriors who served the shogun, the military ruler of Japan. They were Japan's ruling class. In 1868, the shogun lost his power, and the position of samurai was abolished. But the families who had been samurai were still well respected. Kichiko had no brothers to carry on her family's name, so when Rokuichi married her, he took the name Obata. When they adopted Zoroku, he became an Obata, too. Moving in with Rokuichi and Kichiko was not easy for the young boy. He cried on the trip to his new home in Mizusawa, a small village near the ancient city of Sendai.

Though Zoroku was homesick at first, he was excited to have a new grandfather who had been a real samurai warrior. He often pretended that he was a samurai himself. Next to his school was an old castle that had once been the stronghold of samurai lords. It even had a moat! Zoroku and his friends would play there among the cedar trees until school began. One day at home, he took one of the old samurai swords that belonged to his family and pretended to fight a great battle. Unfortunately, his "enemies" were the prized bamboo plants growing in his family's garden!

Rokuichi in his garden at home

6

Despite his wildness, Zoroku enjoyed the quiet work of making art. He showed a talent for painting at a very young age, and even as a five-year-old, he would draw day and night. Maybe he was inspired by his home, which was full of art, and by his adoptive father, who was constantly drawing and painting.

When Zoroku was seven, he began his training in **sumi-e.** This art form uses a type of ink called *sumi* and specially shaped brushes for drawing and painting. *Sumi-e* takes years to learn. For nearly two years, Zoroku painted lines and circles without resting his elbows on the table. It was hard work, but he learned to paint with a steady hand.

Zoroku's wild spirit was calmed as he learned the basic principles of painting. *Sumi-e* is not just a style of brushwork but a way of being. Before beginning a painting, Zoroku tried to make his mind as peaceful as the still waters of a calm lake. He learned to hold himself erect and alert like a hunting heron, and to control his breathing. As he studied plants, birds, and other animals, Zoroku became well trained in using all of his senses. Instead of just looking at his subject, he also touched and smelled it.

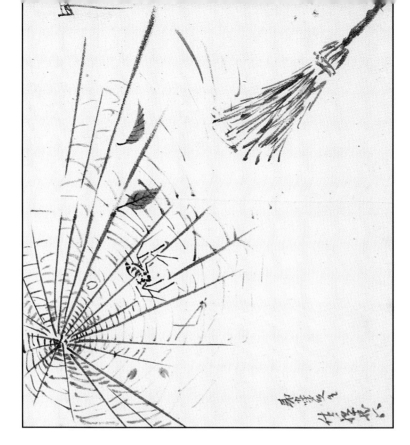

Spider in Cobweb, 1897

Tune in to Nature

Choose a comfortable place where you can observe a natural subject—anything from a hillside to a houseplant. Sit with your back erect, but not stiff. Breathe deeply and hold your breath for a count of three, then slowly release it. As you continue to breathe in this way, begin to tune in to the world around you. Pay attention to what you see, hear, and smell. If you are close to your subject, gently touch it. How do you feel about these sights, sounds, scents, and textures? As you observe nature, practice painting a picture in your mind. Imagine using lines and shapes to sketch your subject, then filling in this outline with color.

Over the years, Zoroku learned from different *sensei*, or master teachers. His first was Chikuson Moniwa. Zoroku practiced painting spiders, fish, houses, and many other things. He became a productive artist like his busy father. Zoroku copied the works of Japan's greatest artists to learn how they painted. He also made little books about his samurai heroes.

Though Zoroku's art got better and better, his behavior didn't. He threw rocks at people who walked by his house. He picked on other kids so much that they ran away when they saw him coming. Only Isoko, Zoroku's grandmother, could control him. She was with him constantly, and he loved her very much.

When Zoroku was fourteen years old, his father enrolled him in a military academy for officer training. Perhaps Rokuichi thought military school would teach his son discipline, but Zoroku rebelled. He wanted to be an artist, not a soldier! With his grandmother's help, he ran away to Tokyo. The city was an exciting place for a young artist in 1899. Not only was it the political capital of Japan, but it was the home of many great Japanese artists at a time when art was changing.

For the past several decades, the Japanese people had been trading with American and European merchants. The Japanese were learning about Western clothes, foods, and art. European oil painting had become popular. Some artists had begun to complain about this change, urging a return to traditional Japanese ink and water-color painting. Others wanted to develop a new style of art, one that blended the old Japanese traditions and the new Western ones. Shortly after Zoroku arrived in Tokyo, he became involved with the artists who were creating this intriguing new way of painting.

Zoroku still had a lot to learn about art. At an art show, he saw the work of a master painter named Tanryo Murata. He decided he wanted Murata to be his *sensei*. Zoroku went to Murata's studio and asked to be his student, but Murata refused. Zoroku didn't give up. Every day, he stood at Murata's door, stubbornly waiting for the artist to change his mind. Finally, Murata sent a letter to Rokuichi, asking him to come to Tokyo to get his son. Even after his father arrived, Zoroku refused to move. Rokuichi politely asked Murata to train his son, and at last the *sensei* agreed. But he had one condition: Zoroku must be a good student.

Zoroku was determined to do his best. At first, Murata made him clean the house and work in the garden. No one would give Zoroku art lessons, so he worked on his own. After one of Zoroku's paintings was accepted in an art show, Murata's assistant began to teach him. As he showed progress, Zoroku was finally taught by the *sensei* himself.

During this time, Zoroku was given a new name. Most students simply took on the name of their *sensei* when they came of age, but Zoroku was renamed by his master. Murata called him Chiura (CHOOL-ruh), which means "a thousand bays," after the beautiful islands near Sendai. So Zoroku's new name was Chiura Obata, and that's how he signed his art.

Chiura (second from left) with some friends as a teenager

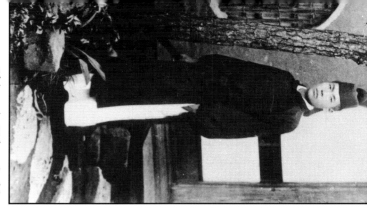

Chiura in Tokyo, in his artist's robes

In 1902, Chiura won third place in an art show for *Early Spring*, a picture of a girl and a blossoming tree. At seventeen, Chiura was the youngest winner at the show. Soon he was offered money to do paintings for people. One showed a samurai lord in full battle dress. Painted on silk with *sumi* and watercolor, it has the detail of a European painting and the fine, delicate lines of the work of his teacher, Tanryo Murata.

By this time, Chiura had been hired to illustrate two books, but he wanted more challenges and adventures. As a painter, he wanted "to respect nature, to melt into nature and find my life in nature." He decided to explore the natural wonders of the United States. Chiura may have had another reason to leave Japan. The nation was about to go to war with Russia. Young men would be drafted, or forced into the army to fight. Perhaps Chiura hoped to seek his fortune and avoid the draft at the same time.

Line Find

In school, Chiura learned three basic brush strokes. The vertical line goes up and down, connecting Earth and sky. The horizontal line brings together right and left; east and west; past, present, and future. The circle is motion. It has no beginning or end.

Supplies

✔ watercolor brush
✔ watercolor paints or ink
✔ paper

What to Do

See what lines you can find. Settle yourself in a comfortable place outdoors and paint any vertical lines you see, such as a tree trunk or falling rain. On a separate sheet of paper, record the horizontal lines you see—a stream or the horizon—by painting them. For a challenge, search for circles (a puddle or a spiderweb) and paint them. Like Chiura, learn to spot the lines in nature. These lines will become the framework of your art.

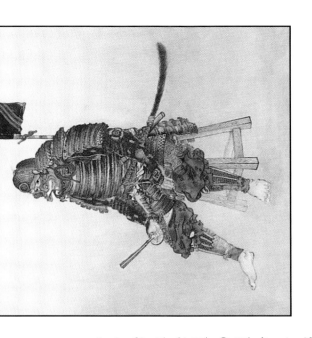

Takeda Clan Samurai, *c. 1902*

Whatever his reasons, Chiura set his sights on California, a place Japanese travel guides depicted as a land of dreams where there was plenty of work and money. In 1903, he sailed to San Francisco. Rokuichi supported Chiura's plans by paying for his passage. Before leaving, Chiura told his father that he would return home "when I am able to create, without fail, masterpieces that will be known to the world as those of Chiura Obata."

Full of hope, Chiura began his new life in San Francisco at the age of seventeen. He entered the Mark Hopkins Art School, but he didn't stay long. After witnessing other students in a food fight, he decided that they must not be very serious about art. He would study on his own. "I felt that I should visit Great Nature myself, and study nature more," he later explained. He began to travel throughout California, "trying to learn something from the heart of nature."

To earn money, he found a job as a "school boy," or servant, for an actor named Edwin Emery. Chiura had little experience doing this sort of work. In Japan, he had been waited on by servants but had never served others. After setting the table on the first night, he sat down between Mr. and Mrs. Emery, held his knife and fork ready, and told Mrs. Emery to cook quickly! Fortunately for Chiura, the Emerys treated him kindly and taught him his job.

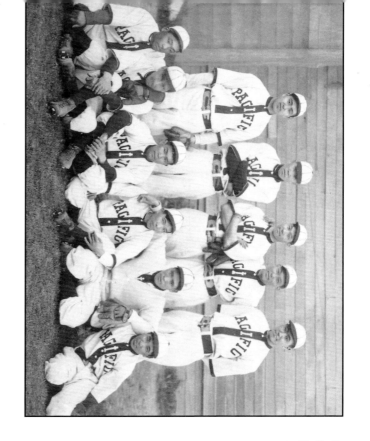

Chiura (seated, second from right) and his baseball teammates

Chiura did not have to work as a servant for long. He found jobs with the city's Japanese newspapers, illustrating articles. He also studied English, but he didn't rush to be successful at learning this new language. He wanted to take time to relax and devote his efforts to studying nature. He was in an excellent spot to do just that. Located on a peninsula between San Francisco Bay and the Pacific Ocean, San Francisco offered quick access to wild beauty. Chiura could easily visit ocean cliffs and open, grassy hills. Just across the Golden Gate—the entrance to San Francisco Bay—stood deep, dark redwood forests.

Chiura didn't spend all his time studying. He was also interested in sports. One day, he watched a baseball game between teams from Waseda University in Japan and Stanford University. Though the Japanese team lost, Chiura was excited about the game. Afterward, he helped organize San Francisco's first Japanese baseball team. Soon there were eight teams, and Chiura played often. He also sprinted and practiced the long jump.

Chiura's good physical condition probably helped prepare him for one of nature's most dramatic events, the San Francisco earthquake of 1906. He awoke at five o'clock one April morning as the chimney crashed into his room. Chiura believed that "you have to face

12

anything that nature gives you with your whole body and spirit." So he grabbed some sketchbooks and walked toward the center of the city to see what was happening. Eager to show how the earthquake affected people, he quickly sketched the terrified citizens who fled past him.

Fires were spreading, so Chiura tried to find an open space where he would be safe. Making a tent with a sheet and string, he was the first one to set up camp in Lafayette Park. Soon others arrived, and Chiura helped some soldiers dig a latrine. An officer noticed how hard he worked and asked if he would wait tables for the officers. Not only did Chiura have a job in the earthquake-ravaged city, but soon he had a pass to go downtown, where only soldiers were allowed. He made over fifty sketches of the devastated area.

San Francisco had been nearly destroyed. Over three thousand people died, and over twenty-eight thousand buildings were wrecked or burned—including Chiura's home. Though he had to camp in the park for six months, he never lost hope. He knew that even when nature is violent, life will endure.

View of Burnt Out Japantown from California Street, *May 18, 1906*

Untitled *(seascape)*, c. 1930

Chapter 2
Art Everywhere

Though California was a land of opportunity, it was also a place where great prejudice—dislike of people of different races or cultures—was growing. Immigrants from all over the world had come to San Francisco over the past several decades. The law allowed all of them to become United States citizens—except those who came from Asia. Most Japanese immigrants worked hard and soon had their own farms and businesses. American workers began to protest that the Japanese immigrants were taking too many jobs. One San Francisco newspaper, the *Chronicle*, started a campaign to send them back to Japan.

Most Japanese experienced prejudice personally, and Chiura was no exception. One day, as he was walking home from a job, he came to a street that was having its cable car rails repaired. When Chiura passed the construction workers, they started calling him names. One slapped him in the face before he could even speak. Though Chiura was humiliated, he decided to stay calm. But when one of the workers spit on him, Chiura hit the man. A fight broke out. Soon the police came, but they arrested only Chiura—not the men who had ganged up on him. Luckily, he knew a good lawyer and had a fair judge. At his trial, the judge set him free, saying that Chiura was only one small painter who had to defend himself against eight big construction workers.

Chiura found relief from incidents like this one by going to wild places such as the seaside. Every New Year's Eve, Chiura went to a beach on the Pacific Ocean. He would dig a pit in the sand, make a cozy fire, and wait for the sunrise. In the morning, he drew his impressions on the wave-pressed sand and imagined the waves carrying his art to his friends and family across the sea in Japan.

Sometimes even wild places weren't free of prejudice. In Japan, being alone with nature was a normal practice, but in the United States, many people considered it strange. One New Year's Eve, Chiura was stopped by a soldier who asked him why he was wandering on the beach in the middle of winter. (Though the country was not at war, the army had stations up and down the coast.) When Chiura explained about drawing in the sand, the soldier didn't believe him. Thinking Chiura was a spy, he took him to the guardhouse. There the captain examined Chiura's sketchbook, which was full of drawings of seagulls and crashing waves, and released him.

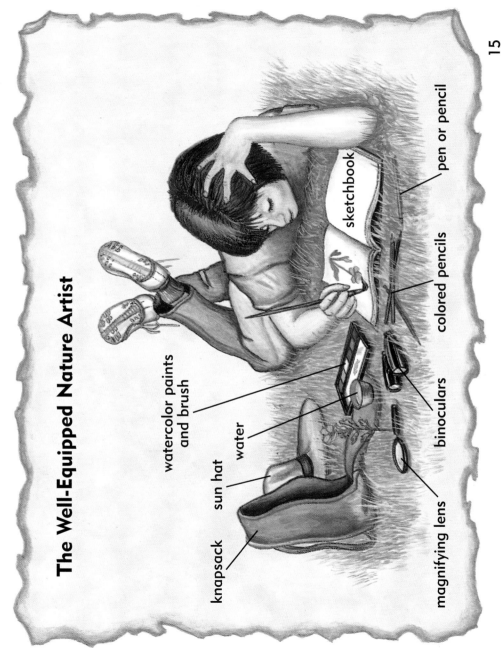

The Well-Equipped Nature Artist

knapsack

sun hat

water

watercolor paints and brush

sketchbook

binoculars

magnifying lens

colored pencils

pen or pencil

Above: Haruko at the beach with son Kimio and daughter Fujiko
Left: Chiura and Haruko's wedding portrait

When Chiura wasn't busy with work or art, he liked to spend time with his many friends in Japantown, the part of San Francisco where many Japanese immigrants lived. At one friend's house, he met a young woman, Haruko Kohashi, who had just come to California and was living with her aunt. Chiura thought she was lovely and cultured. Haruko had been brought up to be a perfect Japanese wife. She was trained in *chanoyu*, the ceremony of serving tea, and *ikebana*, the art of flower arranging. She had come to the United States to learn Western-style sewing and English. Like Chiura, Haruko was strong willed and independent. When her aunt asked her to work at her boardinghouse, Haruko said, "No, I came here to learn how to sew."

On January 7, 1912, Chiura and Haruko were married. Haruko's father gave the young couple a gift of many old, valuable kimonos—silk gowns worn in Japan. In September, Haruko gave birth to their first child, a son named Kimio. Chiura was not only an artist, but a husband and father, too. He worked hard to support his growing family.

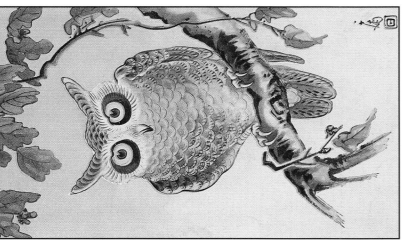

Owl (cover of Japan magazine), December 1921

Chiura's reputation for hard work and beautiful art led to other jobs. This was fortunate, because Haruko gave birth to a daughter, Fujiko, in 1915. Chiura was asked to draw for a travel magazine called *Japan*. Finally he was able to earn money drawing the natural subjects he loved. He painted animals and birds found in Japan, such as the owl and the heron.

Before painting a bird, Chiura looked at it carefully. What shapes were its beak, eyes, and feet? How did it fold its wings and hold its head? By concentrating on the basic construction of the bird, he was able to create pictures that showed the unique character of each **species.** Some of his birds looked so alive, they seemed as if they might even fly off the page!

Bird Portraits

To create fine-feathered art like Chiura's, all you have to do is tune in to the behaviors and bodies of your neighborhood birds.

Supplies
✔ sketchbook, or scratch paper on a clipboard
✔ pen or pencil
✔ colored pencils or crayons

What to Do
✔ Settle yourself in view of a bird feeder, birdbath, or any other place where you often see birds. Focus on a single bird.

✔ Sketch the shape of the bird by making one oval for the body and another for the head.

✔ Look carefully at the shape of the beak, wings, legs, and tail. Add each to the sketch.

✔ Fill in any obvious color patterns that you notice.

✔ For an extra challenge, quickly sketch the bird in different positions, such as flying or hopping.

Though Chiura had become well established as a professional artist, many of his jobs still did not bring him closer to nature. He sometimes got frustrated with painting what other people wanted and stopped working to go fishing. He also continued to take trips throughout California, painting the landscape. Some of his pictures were realistic down to the finest detail. In others, he recorded his impressions with two or three bold strokes of his brush.

One of Chiura's more unusual techniques, which he used in a painting of fog-shrouded redwood trees, was the wet-on-wet application of *sumi* ink. In these pictures, Chiura applied ink to wet paper. The ink would bleed, creating the impression of a foggy day. Chiura used this technique to capture the swirling mist and ever-changing clouds.

Wet-Day Painting

Do you ever wonder what to do on a rainy or misty day? Why not create a piece of wet-day art? As Chiura once said, "You cannot hold a cloud in your pocket, but you can hold your feelings about clouds [by painting them]."

Supplies

✔ several sheets of watercolor paper
✔ newspaper
✔ water
✔ clean sponge or cloth
✔ watercolor paints and brush

What to Do

✔ Choose a place where you can view an interesting outdoor landscape, perhaps one where you can see some trees or hills. Look at the lines of the trees or hills. Can you see how the edges of the lines blur in the rain or fog? Examine the shapes of clouds. What do their outlines look like?

✔ Place your paper on the newspaper. Wipe it with a wet sponge or cloth so the whole surface is moist, but not flooded.

✔ Dip your brush in water. Mix up some watercolor paint until it's about as thick as ink. You don't want it too dry or too wet.

✔ Using single, bold strokes, paint the basic lines that you see. These lines will bleed and give your picture a blurry effect. Experiment with different amounts of moisture on the paper and brush.

✔ Use this technique to try to capture the different clouds you see each time you paint.

Alma, Santa Cruz Mountains,
November 29, 1922

Chiura had friends among San Francisco's other Japanese artists, but he was also interested in being part of a larger community of artists. He believed that "at least in the world of art there shouldn't be any walls between East and West." So Chiura worked with the director of the San Francisco Museum of Art to bring together artists from Asia and the United States. In November of 1922, thirty-seven Japanese, Chinese, American, and Russian artists held a joint art show at the museum under the title of the East West Art Association. This was the beginning of both a new partnership of San Francisco artists and some very important friendships for Chiura.

Despite Chiura's efforts to bring people together, the prejudice against Japanese immigrants grew worse. In February of 1923, the Obatas' son Gyo was born. In 1924, a law was passed that prevented any more Japanese from coming to live in the United States. What would Gyo's future be in a country that didn't want his people? Chiura could only keep working and hope for the best.

Clouds

Clouds are made up of tiny particles of water or ice. They are classified in three main types. Wispy clouds that appear high in the sky are called cirrus. Cumulus clouds are puffy. Clouds that look layered are called stratus. All clouds are variations of these basic types.

The next year, Chiura got a job designing scenery for an opera. When he arrived to start his work, the painter in charge couldn't help doubting him. Chiura had come to paint a background eight feet high and thirty feet long—without a sketch! The painter warned Chiura not to make a mistake. So Chiura quickly painted a large pine tree. The painter was impressed and let Chiura do his job.

Chiura had been able to paint a large pine from memory because he had so much practice in observing trees closely and noticing details. Each time he began to paint, he already had a picture in his mind because he had focused all his senses on his subject.

Greet a Tree

You've probably looked at many trees, but have you ever known one well? Pick a tree in your neighborhood and say hello. Feel its leaves or needles. Touch its bark. Sniff it. Listen to it as it moves with the wind. Carefully observe the texture of your tree's trunk and the position of its branches. What shape are the leaves? What shape is the trunk? Pay close attention to your tree for several days, weeks, or months. When you feel ready, imagine a picture of your tree. Draw the tree without looking at it, then compare your sketch with it. Next, try again, this time looking at the tree. As you continue your tree friendship, keep on sketching. Chances are that your pictures will show how close you've become to your friend dressed in bark.

Pines (genus Pinus)

In the pine family. Over 90 species in the Northern Hemisphere

Habitat: varies. Grows everywhere from seashores to high mountains

Leaves: needles in bundles

Bark: usually flaky

Cones: male and female. Female cones have woody scales. They often reach the size of a baseball, and some are as large as a pineapple. The male cones are the size of a large caterpillar and contain a yellow powder called pollen. Pollen fertilizes mature female cones, causing them to produce seeds called pine nuts.

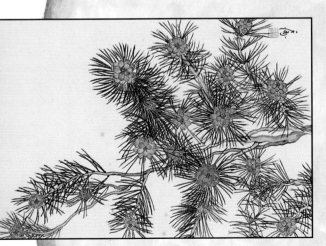

Untitled *(lodgepole pine)*, 1927

Gyo Obata

Yuri Obata

Chapter 3
Mountain Treasures

In April of 1927, Chiura's youngest child was born. Since her birth was so close to Easter, she was named Yuri, which means "lily." Chiura had become the father of four: Kimio, age fourteen; Fujiko, age twelve; Gyo, a rambunctious three-year-old; and baby Yuri.

That summer, Chiura's friend Worth Ryder, an art professor at the University of California in Berkeley, invited him on a long trip to Yosemite National Park. Located in the Sierra Nevada Mountains east of San Francisco, Yosemite was as big as the entire state of Rhode Island. Its waterfalls and mountains were world famous. It would be Chiura's first trip there, and despite the new baby at home, he didn't hesitate to go. Little did he know how much influence the trip would have on his life.

A few weeks later, Chiura and Worth were rumbling along the road to Yosemite in a Model T Ford. They looked like gold seekers. The car was packed with crates of food, cots, fishing gear, a tent, an ax, a shovel, and other camping equipment. Unlike gold miners, however, they also carried sketchbooks and painting supplies.

White Wolf Meadow,
July 4, 1927

As they drove up into the mountains, the landscape changed constantly. The foothills were covered with dried grass the color of a lion's fur. Higher up, the hills became dotted with twisted oaks. At White Wolf, where Chiura and Worth camped for a few days, immense red firs towered over them. Chiura sketched and painted with excitement. He woke early to seek quiet wildflower meadows or views of far mountains.

Partway through the trip, Chiura and Worth were joined by their friend Robert Howard, a sculptor. Chiura told the two men that he intended to paint a hundred pictures during the trip. Later, Robert wrote about what happened the next morning. "[Chiura] disappeared down the trail we had come, and as the sun rose high, groups of hikers began passing, telling of an artist working like mad at the foot of the first falls. As the morning wore on, more hikers passed, each with a word of wonder, till finally along came the artist himself, all fresh and smiling, with a superb painting under his arm."

Yosemite is home to hundreds of different species of wildflowers, and Chiura wished to paint them all. He sketched them, painted them, and even decorated postcards to his family with their bright colors. Chiura studied the delicate blossoms carefully to see how the parts came together to form a whole. Unlike many paintings of plants, Chiura's are not only scientifically accurate, they are as delicate as the flowers themselves. This care shows in his detailed painting of the shooting stars that he saw high in the mountains.

Shooting Stars, July 2, 1927

Shooting Star (genus Dodecatheon)

In the primrose family, which also includes primroses, cyclamens, loosestrifes, and starflowers. There are 15 species of shooting stars in North America.

Habitat: from moist mountain meadows to dry forests and prairies

Flowers: pollinated by bumblebees. Petals point backward, making the flower look like a shooting star.

Fruit: a capsule full of many seeds

Flower Art

Flowers are rich in delicate details. You can explore their intricate parts by picturing them on paper as Chiura did.

Supplies

✔ magnifying lens
✔ paper
✔ pencil
✔ colored pencils or crayons

What to Do

✔ Use your magnifying lens to examine a flower up close. Try sketching, one at a time, some of its parts. With your colored pencils or crayons, try to match the colors that you see. Do you notice any color patterns on the petals? Try to copy them. Focusing on details will help you to draw the whole flower later.

✔ Carefully study how the flower's parts connect. Notice how they are attached to the stem and how the stem comes out of the ground. Where are the leaves attached? Close your eyes and picture what the flower looks like. When you're ready, make a picture of the whole plant.

Chiura's other paintings were also different from those of many artists who had pictured Yosemite. Most of these artists created dramatic landscapes. They captured the towering cliffs, grand mountains, and rocketing waterfalls, but ignored the little things that were also part of the Yosemite experience. Often they focused on dark, stormy scenes. Unlike these artists, Chiura saw art in the simplest scenes as well as in the grandest ones. He filled his paintings with a quiet but beautiful light.

Even Chiura's rocks seemed bright and almost alive. He delighted in sketching and painting the piles of granite boulders that he found throughout the park. With delicate patches of moss and small, twisted trees growing in their cracks, the boulders reminded Chiura of Japanese rock gardens. One day, he sketched granite boulders near White Wolf meadow that were unlike any others in the area. "They have vertical lines like a waterfall and their horizontal lines roar like a lion," he wrote in a letter to Haruko.

Rock Art

There's rock music, so why not rock art? Whether you're holding a small pebble in your palm or leaning against a mammoth boulder, you can become conscious of the basic properties of rocks. For example, unless a rock is molten, like flowing lava, it is solid. Unless it is air-filled, like pumice, it is heavy. What else can you discover about the rocks near your home?

Supplies
- watercolor paints and brush
- paper

What to Do
- Select a rock to study. Place it on each of its sides to see how it sits. Press your hand against it and feel its texture and weight. Put it in water. Do you notice any color changes? Once you tune in to rocks, you may feel more ready to picture them.

- First, create an outline of your rock's shape. Try using heavy bottom lines to show its weight.

- Look for colors and patterns. Try to match them with paint.

- Use a light wash—just a bit of paint on a wet brush—to indicate shadows. Move the rock around to see how the shadows change.

Untitled *(granite rocks), July 2, 1927*

Granite

Granite and granitelike rocks are found all over the world. Granite is an igneous rock formed deep underground. Igneous rocks come from magma—hot, liquid rock—that cools and becomes solid.

True granite is made of equal amounts of a mineral called quartz and two kinds of feldspar, another mineral. Quartz is clear and sparkly. It becomes sand as it breaks down. Feldspar is dull white, pink, blue, or green. It breaks down into fine particles to make clay.

Most rocks that people call granite are really grandodiorites or other granitelike rocks. These rocks are composed of three main minerals: mica, feldspar, and quartz. Mica can be black or clear and is sometimes mistaken for gold.

Though Chiura focused on the small wonders of Yosemite, he didn't ignore its high cliffs and rock domes, which are tall enough to make the Empire State Building look puny. Chiura didn't see the cliffs and domes as part of a huge, dramatic landscape. He focused on the big rocks themselves. In one watercolor, he captured in delicate detail the intricate structure of a large mountain called Half Dome. In another, he used broad brush strokes to convey the immensity of Eagle Peak.

As their adventure came to an end, Chiura, Worth, and Robert chugged up to the high country of Tioga Pass, then down the other side to the sagebrush lands near Mono Lake. Chiura painted the unusual pointed rocks at the top of a volcanic crater and pictured the mountains near Mono Lake that roll toward the horizon like waves. By the end of the two-month trip, he had fulfilled his promise to Worth and Robert by completing 150 pieces of art! Chiura brought home more than his folder of artwork, though. He carried in his heart a new love for Yosemite.

Evening Glow at Yosemite Falls, 1930

In March of 1928, Chiura had his first major, one-person art show in California—a huge honor. Many of his Yosemite watercolors were exhibited, along with selections of his artwork from the previous twenty years. Years ago, Chiura's *sensei*, Tanryo Murata, had told him that "an artist has nothing to say until he has painted at least a thousand paintings." Chiura told a local newspaper that he had selected the show paintings from a collection of more than ten thousand! When the exhibition earned praise from art critics, Chiura felt ready at last to go home to Japan for a visit. He would keep his promise to his father, Rokuichi, to return when his art was known. But on the final day of his exhibition, he got word that his father had just died.

Although Rokuichi wasn't there to greet him, Chiura still decided to return to the land of his birth. In the fall of 1928, he took his entire family to Japan. Chiura brought all his savings to Japan, too. He wanted to have some of his Yosemite watercolors reproduced using an ancient type of Japanese woodblock printing. In this process, a block of wood is carved for each section of color in a painting. The woodblocks are inked and printed, one by one, to create the entire picture. Chiura wanted to use the best materials available for his prints. Special inks had to be made. The paper was made especially for Chiura by a master papermaker. The blocks were carved out of fine cherry wood.

Chiura's project was not only costly but also a tremendous challenge, because his watercolors had such intricate details. It wouldn't be easy to carve pictures of tree branches, boulder-strewn fields, and mountains into blocks of wood. Chiura worked with one of Japan's master printmakers, Tadeo Takamizawa, and a group of eight painters, thirty-two carvers, and forty printers. Although they were the best printmakers in Japan, Chiura was not pleased with the initial results. The colors didn't look at all like the colors he had seen in the Sierra Nevada. They looked "as if the High Sierra had gone on a trip to Japan," Chiura said later. The printmakers had used the colors of Japanese nature and art. How could he show them that California looked different?

Chiura took the group to eat at a fine restaurant. There, he described the Sierra down to the last details of the rocks and trees. The printmakers tried again. The second attempt was better, and on the third try, Chiura was satisfied at last. They had begun with thirty-five paintings and made four hundred prints of each. Chiura kept only the best one hundred prints of each painting. Thousands of prints whose colors didn't turn out perfectly were destroyed. Perhaps it was because of this perfectionism that one of the woodblock prints, *Lake Basin in the High Sierra*, won first place in the 1928 Annual Exhibition of Japanese art in Tokyo.

Lake Basin in the
High Sierra, *1930*

Chiura (third from right, seated), Haruko (second from left, seated), and their children with family members in Japan

After two years in Japan, the Obata family was ready to return to the United States. (Fujiko, who had been invited to live with Haruko's mother and sister, stayed behind.) Back in California, artists and art critics alike were thrilled by the woodblock prints. Viewers understood and marveled at the skill and patience of the printmakers. But more importantly, people everywhere were stirred by the feelings Chiura's paintings reflected. Said one art critic, "To see our native beauty spots through the eyes of a foreign artist . . . is to find charm in our own land." Another called Chiura "a nature worshiper if there ever was one." Chiura was more than pleased. He had earned high praise from art critics in both his native land and his adopted home of California.

Chiura often taught his art classes outdoors.

Chapter 4
Sensei Obata

In 1932, Chiura's career took a new path. He was invited to teach summer classes at the University of California in Berkeley, where his friend Worth Ryder taught. Chiura's *sumi-e* classes were probably the first ever taught at a university outside Japan. The students loved them, and the university hired Chiura full-time. Some people at the university objected to his employment because he didn't have a college degree or even a high school diploma. But Chiura was supported by his friends in the art department, who saw him as a master painter and teacher.

Chiura's students quickly realized he was no ordinary art teacher, especially when they found out what he used for painting. Following recipes over a thousand years old, he mixed rich colors from semiprecious stones, oyster shells, and other gifts of nature. His *sumi* ink came from the mountains of Japan. His brushes were handmade from the fur of animals such as rabbits, foxes, sheep, and bears. Even his water was chosen for its purity—he often carried jugs of water home from his trips to Yosemite! With these ancient techniques and tools, Chiura created new and different art.

Students Sketching at
Faculty Glade, *c. 1935*

As a teacher, Chiura always shared his intense love and respect for nature. He believed that every person could find truth, beauty, and peace in the natural world, and he cared more about teaching his students to see beauty than training them in specific painting skills. Chiura also reminded his students not to imitate other artists, but to picture nature as they saw it. He often took them outdoors to the lovely wooded area along Strawberry Creek on the university campus. There, he asked them to sit and carefully observe everything around them—especially the coast live oak trees, which had dark, twisting branches and rich, green crowns. On very hot days, Chiura took the students into the shade of these trees to sketch tree trunks and shadows. Later he would ask them to draw the scene from memory.

Chiura often taught his students through stories, such as the tale of a poor fisherman's son who became blind. The boy was so upset that he wanted to drown himself. He was about to drown himself in a moat when he heard his mother's voice. "You are my son," she said, "but you also belong to nature, and nature gave you blindness." Taking courage from these words, the boy studied and grew into a great artist. His inner sight became greater than the outward vision of others. Chiura encouraged his students to shed fear as the blind man had done, so that they, too, could develop their inner sight.

Shadow Catcher

Though Peter Pan's shadow could be caught, most shadows can be held only in pictures. Here's how to catch a few shadows with paint.

Supplies
✔ dark blue or black watercolor paint
✔ watercolor brush
✔ paper

What to Do
✔ Sit in the shade of a tree on a day when the air is like a hot oven. Feel the coolness of the shade. Study the shadows, paying attention to the varying shades of darkness you see. Which is darker, the tree's trunk or its shadows? When you feel ready, start painting.

✔ Use the fine tip of your brush for thin lines like branches.

✔ Experiment with broad, steady strokes for the sturdy trunk.

✔ To paint shadows, get the brush wet and use just a bit of dark blue or black paint. This wet mixture will create a shadowy-looking wash.

Coast Live Oak (genus Quercus)

Belongs to the beech family. The coast live oak is one of over 600 species of oaks in the world. It is called a live oak because it keeps its leaves all winter.

Leaves: dark green and glossy. May have small spines on edges

Bark: dark gray and checkered

Habitat: coastal hills from northern California to Baja California

Flowers: has male and female catkins (dangling flowers) that hang from the branches in spring

Like a wizard of brush and paint, Chiura showed his classes how to make art. The challenge of painting a fast-swimming goldfish, he said, is to get the feel of the fish from its basic shape to its sparkling scales. This difficulty could be met by sharpening one's senses like the pointed tip of a fine brush. Chiura's students had plenty of chances to do just that. They observed animals in the zoo, birds flying around Berkeley, and even the slimy garden snail. Chiura tuned students in to the fall of a dewdrop, the springing leap of a dog, and the flow of a bubbling brook. With quick, light brush strokes, he taught students how to picture not only natural subjects, but also the way they moved.

Moving Pictures

In the early days of Hollywood, movies were called moving pictures. With a video camera, you can easily capture the art of movement, but you can also use a brush, paint, and paper.

Supplies

- pencil
- paper
- watercolor brush
- watercolor paints or ink

What to Do

- Study nature in motion—a stalking cat, a leaf blowing in the wind, or a burbling brook. Use a pencil to sketch your subject, then add paint.

- Create the appearance of speed with a quick brush stroke, or add slowness and weight with heavy colors and lines.

- Play with balance. Paint a leaning tree as though it's about to fall off the paper, or sketch a leaping frog in midair.

Garden Snails (subclass Prosobranchia)

Range: found all over the world
Diet: leaves and other plant parts
Eggs: may lay 50 eggs at a time

Untitled (*snail*), *c. 1950*

Life was good for Chiura and his family. Although the United States was in a severe economic depression and many people were out of work, he had a good job. The Obatas' home was always a busy place. Chiura taught private lessons as well as his university classes. Haruko kept busy teaching *ikebana*, and they both lovingly tended a Japanese garden. The house was often full of students and friends, both Japanese and American. Still, Chiura loved his solitude. At least once a week, he would escape the commotion altogether and go surf fishing on the Pacific coast.

Every summer, the entire family traveled up to Yosemite to camp near the Merced River. Chiura's students would join them, and Chiura spent his time painting, teaching, and fishing. He would also visit with his close friend Ansel Adams. Ansel was a photographer whose incredible pictures were making Yosemite known throughout the world. Chiura had known him since the early days of the East West Art Association, and Ansel often exhibited Chiura's art in the studio he ran with his wife, Virginia. The two artists often influenced one another's work. Adams captured Chiura in a photo as a peaceful Yosemite fisher. Chiura pictured Ansel in a quick sketch. One time, Ansel even dashed off to photograph a waterfall after seeing how Chiura had captured a unique view of it in a painting.

Ansel Adams's portrait of Chiura

33

These were peaceful times, but peace was not on the horizon. In the 1930s, Japan began to take over parts of China and other nearby countries. The United States controlled some territories in Asia, so many Americans were concerned about Japan's actions. In California, where most Japanese immigrants lived, resentment and harassment of the immigrants increased. When Kimio graduated with a master's degree in art and design in 1939, he couldn't get a job. Instead, he ended up managing an art store and studio that his parents owned.

Chiura was distressed, too. In the spring of 1941, he and other Berkeley professors were invited to a secret meeting with Milton Eisenhower, a government official from Washington, D.C. Chiura learned that the government was worried about the loyalty of Japanese Americans. Some officials wanted to put them on reservations, similar to those where Native Americans had been sent to live. Chiura argued against this idea. He assured Eisenhower that if the United States went to war against Japan, his people would be loyal to the country they had chosen as their home.

Half a year later, on December 7, Japanese planes attacked the American naval base in Pearl Harbor, Hawaii. The United States declared war against Japan. Anti-Japanese feelings raged throughout California. Someone even fired a bullet through the front window of the Obatas' art store. Chiura and Haruko had to shut the store and cancel classes. Chiura felt like his world was sliding into a vortex, like a funnel of water draining from a bathtub. He expressed this feeling of helplessness in a swirling, spinning painting entitled *Landslide*.

Landslide, 1941

Tree in Storm, c. 1942

Chapter 5
Storm Tree

In February of 1942, President Franklin Roosevelt signed an order that allowed the military to intern, or imprison, "enemy aliens," people who came from countries with which the United States was at war. At the time, 110,000 people of Japanese ancestry lived on the West Coast. The military decided to intern the West Coast Japanese Americans in camps. (The Japanese Americans who lived in the eastern United States were spared, because they were far from the military operations on the West Coast.) Everyone sent to the internment camps would have to give up their homes, businesses, and jobs.

For the Obatas, the order meant the end of Berkeley art classes, trips to Yosemite, and their busy, happy home. Each person was allowed to take only a single suitcase. Haruko immediately began packing the family's belongings and taking them to friends for safekeeping. Chiura was very upset. Instead of helping Haruko, he busied himself with a painting of a giant sequoia in a snowstorm. Later he wrote a caption to go with the painting: "Whipped by spring rain, burned with summer's heat, slashed by lightning, buffeted by wind, burdened by winter's blanket of snow, rocked by Earth's shakings and slides, resisting a host of enemies, the old tree slowly reaches toward eternal beauty." Perhaps Chiura imagined that he and his family would be that tree.

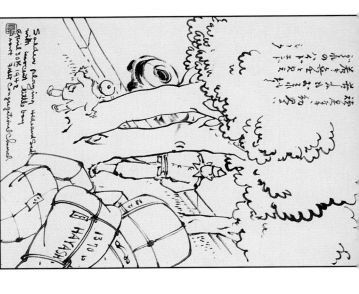

Left: Soldier Playing Hide and Seek with Innocent Little Boy, April 30, 1942
Right: Finding New Dwellings, April 30, 1942

Gyo was in school at Berkeley and wanted to continue his studies. He insisted that he would not go to the internment camp. He thought the camps were against the principles of the United States government, which was founded on the belief that people should be free. The government wanted to lock up the Obatas, even though they hadn't been convicted of a crime. Their only crime was being of Japanese ancestry. Fortunately, a friend helped Chiura get permission for Gyo to attend school in St. Louis, Missouri. Chiura himself chose to stay. "I decided the best thing for me was to help and support my people in this trying time," he said later.

The Obatas became internees on April 30, 1942. From the very first day, as they were herded into buses by soldiers, Chiura recorded the story of their imprisonment. With *sumi* brush and ink, he sketched a small boy playing hide-and-seek with a young soldier. He drew a farewell picture of the Bay Bridge. He painted an old, blind man struggling through the rain and mud to his new home—a horse stall at the abandoned racetrack called Tanforan that was now the internees' jail.

Tanforan was a temporary camp, located south of San Francisco, where the internees were kept until more permanent camps could be built. Japanese-American families, who had been proud of their

36

clean, neat homes, were herded into stalls like horses. Haruko burst out crying when she saw the stall's rough walls and smelled its nasty odor. This was their home? There were no windows and no heat. The family had to sleep on bags filled with straw, and it was a long walk to the common bathroom. Only Yuri, who loved horses, saw the experience as an adventure.

Chiura turned his heart toward his art and his people. He knew that they must maintain their pride and continue to see the beauty in nature to survive. Right away, he began to organize an art school and was made its director by the camp authorities. Chiura found teachers in the other artists, many his own students, who had also been interned. With the help of friends outside the camp, they got basic supplies and scavenged other materials from the camp itself. Soon hundreds of people were taking classes. They carved sculptures from tree stumps, built lamps from old car parts, and made hats from reeds that grew in a nearby marsh. Chiura offered classes in *sumi-e*, landscape painting, and dozens of other art techniques. He wrote, "In any circumstance, anywhere, anytime, take up your brush and express what you face and what you think without wasting your time and energy complaining and crying."

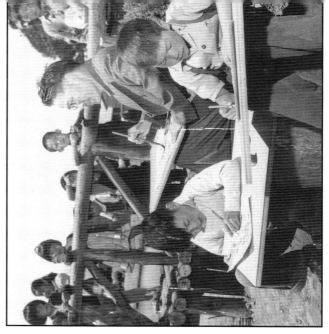

Left: One of the horse stalls where Tanforan residents lived
Right: Chiura teaches art at Tanforan.

Although Chiura wasn't happy about his new life, he kept his sense of humor. For lunch, the internees were served "pork and beans" without any pork. In a booming voice, Chiura called this skimpy meal "beans and beans." The Obatas later learned that camp officials were taking some of the food money. The food improved when the government brought in new officials to run the dining hall.

Chiura also showed his spirit when his non-Japanese-American students came to visit. Because the camp had only a small room for visiting, Chiura's students sometimes had to stand at the edge of the camp and talk to him through the fence. They would cry when they saw their former professor's imprisonment. "From my perspective it looks like *you* are behind the fence," he told them.

Talking through the
Wire Fence, July 1942

Feel Your Art

When Chiura's heart was stormy, he would paint a storm. When he felt calm, he might picture a placid lake or a fine sunset. Like Chiura, you can let your moods find a voice in your art. Look for symbols in nature that speak the feelings inside you. If you're feeling lonely, you might paint a lone hawk in the sky. If you feel joyful, you might sketch a bursting, bubbling fountain in a garden of flowers. As Chiura taught his students at Tanforan, the most important thing is to follow your feelings. You don't need expensive brushes or fancy paints—any materials you have on hand can be used to express your mood.

After a wet spring and a soggy summer, the residents of Tanforan were transferred to new camps. In September of 1942, the Obatas arrived at Topaz Detention Center in the heart and heat of Utah's Sevier Desert. Not only was the temperature 110°F, but there was dust everywhere. When the wind blew, the internees had to cover themselves with blankets, even indoors. As at Tanforan, the quarters were small. Families of ten or more people crammed themselves into spaces the size of an average bedroom.

Mount Topaz, named for the gem found on its flanks, stood on the western horizon. Living behind a barbed-wire fence in the desert was no one's idea of home, but Chiura saw beauty even in this landscape. "Everyone was always complaining, but Chiura would say, 'Just look around,'" Haruko remembered years later. He sketched carp found in a ditch, drew delicate pictures of garden plants, and even made a detailed picture of a scorpion.

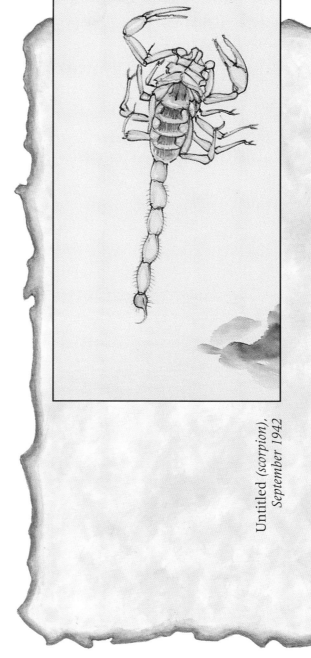

Untitled (scorpion), September 1942

Scorpions (order Scorpiones)

Related to spiders and ticks. Over 1,200 species in the world

Habitat: most are found in warm places, but some are found high up in the Alps and the Andes Mountains. Usually live under stones or logs

Diet: insects and spiders. Use stinger for killing prey and defense

Young: ride on mother's back until big enough to live independently

Chiura also created watercolors of the desert and the camp that celebrated the pale colors and barren landscape. One of these paintings was sent to the White House as a gift. It must have been strange for Chiura to receive a thank-you note from the First Lady, Eleanor Roosevelt, addressed to him at an internment camp.

Chiura helped those around him see beauty in the desert, too. On one trip to the mountains to collect firewood, he and his fellow workers discovered naturally dwarfed trees, which the Japanese call *bonsai*. The group carefully dug up the tiny trees, brought them back to Topaz, and created Japanese-style gardens next to their barracks. Slowly, the internees tried to fill their lives with beauty.

As at Tanforan, Chiura soon founded an art school and became its director. He took advantage of this position to urge that living conditions be improved. Unfortunately, little changed. With crowding, poor food, and difficult weather, life at Topaz was a challenge. It became even more challenging when internees were asked to sign oaths swearing allegiance to the United States government. This issue immediately divided the community. Those opposed to signing the oath were called the No Nos. They argued that it was crazy to give allegiance to a country that had imprisoned them for no reason other than their ancestry. The Yes Yesses, on the other hand, believed that life would improve once they showed their loyalty by signing the oath. They felt they had no choice but to sign.

Chiura's home was California, and he wanted to be a United States citizen. He decided to sign the oath. Many of the No Nos focused their anger on people who, like Chiura, cooperated with the officials who ran the camp. One night, Chiura was attacked and hit on the head with an iron pipe. The wound required ten stitches and several days in the hospital.

The government had begun to allow internees who signed the oath to leave for cities in the Midwest and the East. To protect Chiura from future attacks, the government gave the Obatas permission to settle in St. Louis, where Gyo was in school. Chiura and Kimio found jobs at a commercial art company. The family was happy to leave behind the camp for a community where they would be treated with respect. Still, Chiura waited anxiously for the day he could return to his home and work in Berkeley, where the university had kept his job waiting for him.

By 1945, Japan had begun to lose the war. It was difficult to get news from overseas, and some time passed before the Obatas got the sad word that Fujiko had died of illness in April. In August, when the United States dropped two atomic bombs on the Japanese cities of Hiroshima and Nagasaki, the war ended. Like most people, Chiura was shocked by the destruction. His three atomic bomb paintings show his changing feelings. The first painting is called *Devastation*, the second, *Prayer*, and the last, which shows grass growing from the wreckage, *Harmony*. Chiura hoped the paintings would show the balance between life and death, destruction and growth—a balance he had seen in his own life over the course of the war.

Prayer, 1945

Chapter 6
Home at Last

Chiura paints in King's Canyon National Park in August of 1948.

In October of 1945, the Obatas returned to Berkeley. Chiura resumed his life as a teacher and artist without bitterness. The war years were behind him. Ahead lay more adventures. He continued to visit Yosemite and other places sacred to him. He took camping trips with the Sierra Club, an organization formed to protect wild places. One of the Sierra Club's rules was to burn only dead wood for campfires. Once, when Chiura was camped near a high meadow in the southern Sierra, he realized that even this rule was not right. In front of him stood a beautiful tree that had been struck dead by lightning. Above the lifeless tree the moon shone, and between its branches sparkled a mountain. Within the dead tree, Chiura saw live beauty shining. At the campfire, he shared his thoughts on the sacredness of this dead tree and asked that it be spared. No one cut it. Perhaps it's still there.

In 1952, Chiura's wish to become an official American was granted. The citizenship laws had been changed, and Chiura was finally allowed to become a citizen of the country he had lived in for almost half a century. As he had hoped, things had gotten better for his people and himself.

Throughout his teaching years, Chiura had found time to go fishing. In 1954, he retired from teaching and had even more time for this hobby. He often prepared his catch as a raw fish dish called *sashimi*. Sometimes, before eating the fish, he would sketch it. Other times, he might make a fish print by covering the dead fish with paint, then pressing it between pieces of paper. This left an impression of the outline and textures of the fish. One print of a large striped bass hung on the wall of Chiura's house.

Nature Prints

You can make prints like Chiura did by using fish, leaves, branches, or any other natural objects.

Supplies
✔ newspaper
✔ watercolor or poster paints
✔ paintbrush
✔ paper

What to Do
✔ Set the object on some newspaper, then apply paint to the object with your brush.

✔ Place a sheet of paper on top. Press down with the palms of your hands. For a different texture, rub a finger back and forth over the paper.

✔ Try making a print by sandwiching the painted object between two pieces of paper.

Striped Bass (*Morone saxatilis*)

Part of the sea bass family, which has about 400 species. Largest are over 6 feet long and 125 pounds in weight. Can live for 25 years

Habitat: native to the Atlantic Ocean. Introduced to the Pacific in 1879 as game fish. Live close to the ocean floor and often rest there

Diet: insects, mussels, crustaceans, menhaden, herring, and other small fish

Reproduction: spawns, or breeds, between March and July

Untitled (*striped bass*), September 24, 1934

Since the time he had helped to organize the East West Art Association, Chiura had believed that greatness and peace would come from people joining together in harmony. As an old man, he wanted to continue to share his belief in nature and peaceful living. Just as he was thinking about taking a trip to Japan to see his family and friends, he was asked by a travel agency to lead tours there. The agency wanted him to teach Americans about Japanese culture. Chiura gladly accepted the offer. He led tours each autumn and spring for the next twelve years. While on tour, he shared his knowledge of Japanese culture, especially art, and his people's love of nature.

At the age of eighty, Chiura received the Order of the Sacred Treasure, an award given by the Japanese emperor, for promoting peace and understanding between the United States and Japan. In his mid-eighties, Chiura published two books, one about *sumi-e* and another about traveling in Japan. Not long after this, he had a stroke, a blockage of blood to the brain. Chiura could still paint and fish, but he gradually retreated into his past. He rarely spoke English. He enjoyed his garden, especially watching the growth of the rare dawn redwood that a fellow professor, Ralph Cheney, had given him.

On October 6, 1975, Chiura died peacefully of old age. He left us his rich art and these words: "Immerse yourself in nature, listen to what nature tries to tell you in its quietness, that you can learn and grow." Follow the path of nature artist Chiura Obata and have a peaceful and awe-inspiring journey!

Chiura in 1968, creating a sumi-e painting. Haruko watches in the background.

Important Dates

1885—Zoroku Sato is born on November 18 on the island of Honshu in Japan.

1890—Adopted by older brother Rokuichi and his wife, Kichiko. Last name changes to Obata

1899—Studies in Tokyo. Given new name, Chiura, by *sensei*

1902—Wins third prize in art competition

1903—Moves to San Francisco

1906—Sketches San Francisco earthquake. Works as illustrator

1912—Marries Haruko Kohashi. Son Kimio born

1915—Begins illustrating for *Japan* magazine. Daughter Fujiko born

1921—Helps found East West Art Association in San Francisco

1923—Son Gyo born

1927—Daughter Yuri born. Goes on sketching trip to Yosemite

1928—Father dies. Returns to Japan and makes woodblock prints

1930—Returns to California. Has one-person art shows in California and Hawaii

1932—Appointed art instructor at University of California at Berkeley

1942—Interned at Tanforan, then moves to Topaz Relocation Center

1943—Released from Topaz. Moves to St. Louis

1945—Daughter Fujiko dies. Returns to teaching at Berkeley

1952—Becomes United States citizen

1954—Retires from teaching. Leads first tour to Japan

1965—Receives Order of the Sacred Treasure from Japanese emperor

1975—Dies on October 6

Glossary

naturalist: a person who studies nature

samurai: a member of a warrior class that existed in Japan prior to 1868

sensei: master teachers

species: a type of plant or animal with common traits

sumi-e: a type of painting done with ink and special brushes

Chiura caught this brown trout in the John Muir Wilderness in August of 1947.

Bibliography

Fujii, Masuji, translated by Kimi Hill and Akiko Shibagaki. "Chiura Obata: An Oral History." Japanese American History Project, University of California at Los Angeles Special Collections Library. Photocopy.

Hill, Kimi. "Chiura Obata: Biography: Internment and Relocation During World War II." Unpublished manuscript.

Hill, Kimi. Conversations with author, January 1997 and February–June 1999.

Hill, Kimi. "Oral History of Haruko Obata." Transcribed from Japanese by Yuri Kodani.

Houston, Jeanne Wakatsuki, and James D. Houston. *Farewell to Manzanar.* Boston: Houghton Mifflin Company, 1973.

Ichioka, Yuji. *The Issei: The World of the First Generation Japanese Immigrants, 1885–1924.* New York: The Free Press, 1988.

Kodani, Yuri. Conversations with author, January 1997.

Kodani, Yuri. Written recollections of Chiura Obata's trip to Yosemite, 1996.

Obata, Chiura. Papers. Obata family archives, Berkeley, California.

Obata, Chiura. *Sumi-e.* Berkeley, Calif.: Self-published, 1967.

O'Brien, David J., and Stephen S. Fugita. *The Japanese American Experience.* Bloomington, Ind.: Indiana University Press, 1991.

Yosemite Association. *Obata's Yosemite: The Art and Letters of Chiura Obata from His Trip to the High Sierra in 1927.* Yosemite, Calif.: Yosemite Association, 1993.

All quotations in this book are taken from the above sources.

Index